MW00892342

We Are Gobsmacked British Sweary

an adult coloring book of british swear words and slang

100% Original Art

Mix Books, LLC

mix-booksonline.com

The British tend to have a more casual approach to swearing than their American counterparts. Expletives are used quite frequently, though often in humor rather than vulgarity, with the original meanings either forgotten or ignored. With that in mind, here is an explanation of these "Britishisms" and slang you will be coloring:

Bampot: This is Scottish slang that can run the gamut from "trouble-maker" to "simpleton" to "crazy." Possibly related to "barmpot." Barm is the head of a beer and is sometimes used to describe a feeble-minded person, as in "barmy."

Bawbag: A word with its origins in mans' most private parts, which is slang for a stupid or annoying person.

Bint: An insulting way to describe a woman who is considered classless. *"Look…you can't proclaim yourself king just because some moistend bint lobbed a scimitar at you." – Monty Python and the Holy Grail.*

Blimey o' Reilly: A mild expression of surprise and disbelief, on a par with "Well, I never" or "Who'd 'ave believed it?" We have no idea who first coined this Irish phrase but it's the sort of thing you might say if you saw three little old ladies stealing silverware off the café table at tea time. *Also see "Cor Blimey."*

Bloody Hell: Probably the most well-known of British slang and the most versatile. It's used to express everything from dismay or surprise to anger and disgust. As an expletive bloody hell has been used for centuries though its origin is unclear. Most likely, "bloody" was derived from "God's blood" (some say the blood of Christ on the cross) and would have been considered quite profane. Adding "hell," once a taboo subject, would have made the expression quite blasphemous. In today's UK, "bloody hell" is used as casually as "darn." Heck, it's even liberally used in a Harry Potter movie.

Bollocks: Here we go with the male body parts again. This time it's the testicles and the word is used figuratively to mean "nonsense," or might also describe something that's poor quality – "That medieval show was a load of bollocks," or could be synonymous with "bloody hell." Perhaps the oldest word on this list, "bollocks (ballokes)" was used in its true sense in the 14th century but by the mid-1600s it had acquired coarser meaning.

Bugger: Nowadays Bugger is used as an all-around word of annoyance, as in "Oh bugger! There are no olives for my martini." In some parlance it could refer to a contemptible man; conversely you may hear it spoken in an endearing way: "That toddler's a cute little bugger, isn't he?" This is rather ironic as its earlier meaning was synonymous with sodomite, the word coming from the French "bougre," denoting a heretic.

Bugger off: A not so polite way of saying "Please go away."

Cobblers: Cobblers actually has nothing to do with shoemakers. It comes from Cockney rhyming slang, where expressions are substituted for rhyming words. In this case, "cobblers' awls" rhymes with "balls," and over time the full expression has been shortened to "cobblers." The word is often used in phrases like, "That's a load of cobblers." It should also be mentioned that the balls in question are not the bouncy rubber kind – get it?

Codswallop – Nowadays means nonsense as in a person saying, "I'm a really good darts player," but when he keeps missing the board his friend replies, "That's codswallop."
     The most widely touted origin of this term is the story of Hiram Codd. He developed a technique for bottling and sealing fizzy drinks using a glass stopper, which not unreasonably was called the Codd bottle. Beer – a fizzy drink – was known as "wallop," hence "codswallop." But as we said, this *is* a story.

Cor Blimey: An expression of astonishment, thought to derive from "God blind me," spoken when a person saw something they shouldn't have. Sometimes spelled and spoken as "gorblimey." Nowadays used to express surprise or sometimes annoyance and often just used as "Blimey."

Daft Cow: A belittling phrase applied to a stupid woman. Probably first spoken by a farmer to his wife when she knocked over the milk pail (we just made that up). In typical British fashion, Daft Cow can also be used as an endearment or playful term, such as "Look at you, you daft cow."

Dog's Dinner: You will generally hear this in a phrase like, "She was done up like the dog's dinner." And once again, it can have completely opposite meanings. The most accepted use is when a woman tries to dress to impress but makes a complete hash of it. There are some, on the other hand, who use it to describe a smartly dressed lady. If you've ever paid attention to the typical dinner a dog eats, this may seem senseless until we tell you the phrase could be derived from "to put on the dog," which was used in the late 1800s to describe someone who dressed ostentatiously.

Duffer: An incompetent, clumsy or plodding person, sometimes unkindly used to describe old people. The Scots used the word "dowfart" for a stupid person and "douf" for spiritless. "Duffer" may be a derivation of these terms and was in use by the mid-19th century.

Gentleman Sausage: More properly a "Gentleman's Sausage," a rather polite way of referring to a man's proudest private part.

Gobsmacked: If you are gobsmacked you're shocked speechless. (We couldn't have the queen saying anything nasty, could we?). In 1980s Britain you might have been told to shut your gob, gob meaning mouth. Gobsmacked is thought to relate to slapping your hand across your mouth when surprised.

Gormless: A word to describe a clueless dimwit. Thought to be a variant of the old English "gaum," meaning understanding.

How's your father: Simply put – sex. To put it in context, you might hear someone ask, "Where's Bill?" To which his friend replies, "He's having a bit of How's Your Father." Frequently, the reply will be accompanied by a lewd expression or obscene hand gesture, or both.

The origin of this phrase is unsure. One school of thought has it that it was the catchphrase of a vaudeville entertainer who used it in his skits. How it came to be codified for sex is anyone's guess. A more entertaining, though bizarre, suggestion comes from Victorian fathers' desire to protect their daughters' virginity. The dads would hide beneath the young ladies' voluminous skirts. When a suitor approached in hopes of getting close, he would politely ask, "How is your dear father?" If dear dad was between the girl's legs, she would cast her eyes down and say something like, "He is well, thank you, and continues to pursue his interest in methods of castration," which the beau would of course understand as "Not now, Henry."

Jebend: A colossal berk. (Oh, a berk is a contemptuous fool and a good description for Punch in the Jebend and Bint illustration). Let's explain here. There's a popular puppet show in Britain, frequently performed on the beach, that features Punch, a hooked-nosed, hunchbacked and sometimes cruel character. His nemesis is Judy who is a relentless nag and has a baby. Not surprisingly, the show is called Punch and Judy and kids find it hysterically funny, especially when Punch and Judy toss the baby around or Punch kills other puppet characters. Hey, we're just telling it like it is.

My Blooming Arse: Fast track to the movie, *My Fair Lady*, and a scene at the race course where Eliza shrieks out to the horse Dover, "Move yer bloomin' arse," and shocks the high society of the day. Originally, the word was bloody, not bloomin,' but nowadays you will hear people say, "my blooming arse," as an expression of surprise or annoyance, akin to "I'll be a monkey's uncle."

Numpty: Popular in Scotland, means "idiot," or "dope," and comes from "numps," an old word for a stupid person.

Pillock: Thought to come from a 16th century Norse word, pillicock, meaning penis. The Vikings may have meant it as a certain body part, but it took the Brits to corrupt it and use it as an insult when referring to a stupid person. To emphasize a person's stupidity, you might call them a "complete pillock."

Piss off: Another way of saying "Get lost." Piss originates from the French, pissier, to urinate.

Scrubber: Today refers to a vulgar, promiscuous woman. You probably think it originally referred to a scullery maid or cleaner who scrubbed floors. Wrong! Most likely it comes from "scrub," a word that's been in use since the 18th century describing someone who had to scrape around for money and food, and resort to prostitution.

Sod off: Same meaning as bugger off. The word sod is derived from the biblical city of Sodom, where people supposedly engaged in consensual sexual acts considered taboo at the time.

Spunktrumpet: Sometimes written as "spunk trumpet," which makes the meaning a little more obvious. If you haven't guessed it yet, it's referring to a particular appendage on a man as a musical instrument.

Tosspot: A drunk or loathsome swine. Goes back to the 16th century (again!) and was even used by Shakespeare. Believed to have its origin in drunks tossing back too much ale.

Trollop: A lady of loose morals; a prostitute. This may have derived from another 16th century word, the German trulle that referred to a prostitute, or possibly a troll. (OK, we can sort of see that connection).

Twonk: Slightly worse than calling someone an idiot. You might say, "Only a twonk would bungee jump from Big Ben."

There are various theories on where twonk came from, ranging from a word applied to foreigners in the Victorian era to a combination of "twit" and "plonker" originating in the 1980s, but no hard evidence appears to exist.

Useful as tits on a bull: This is pretty self-evident. After all, what use *are* tits on a bull? However, as usual the Brits can't keep things simple; you will often hear "Use*less* as tits on a bull." The first version has more of a note of sarcasm to it, though the general meaning is the same. And in case you're wondering about the character in our illustration, he is John Bull, the personification of the British nation just as Uncle Sam is to the USA.

Wanker: In brief, a masturbator. In more general terms a guy who is decidedly unpleasant. In our illustration, the wanker is a grenadier guard, surprised in the act so that the hair on his beaver fur hat stands on end.

Wankstain: An odious waste of space. Take a look at the description for Wanker, and this will become quite clear.

Wazzock: A stupid dimwit, such as a policeman oblivious to the mugging of an old lady behind his back. Possibly a more recent insult from the north of England, and a contraction of "wiseacre" (a know-it-all) but we prefer another story. Medieval kings would take a crap on a shovel, then the royal dung would be thrown, or "wazzed" outside. "Wazzock" was the term for the shovel.

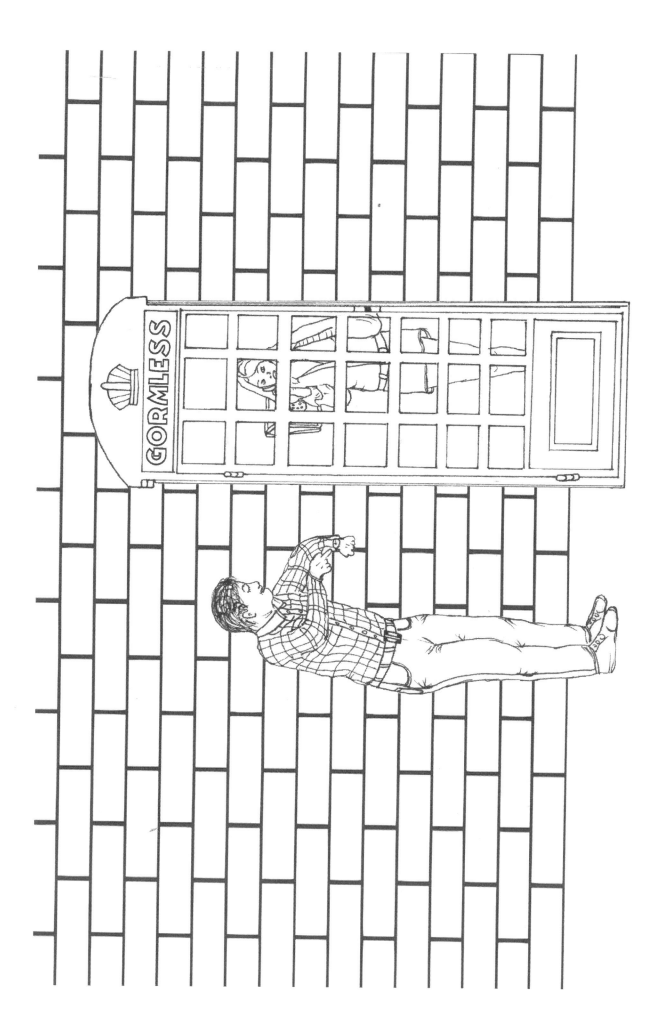

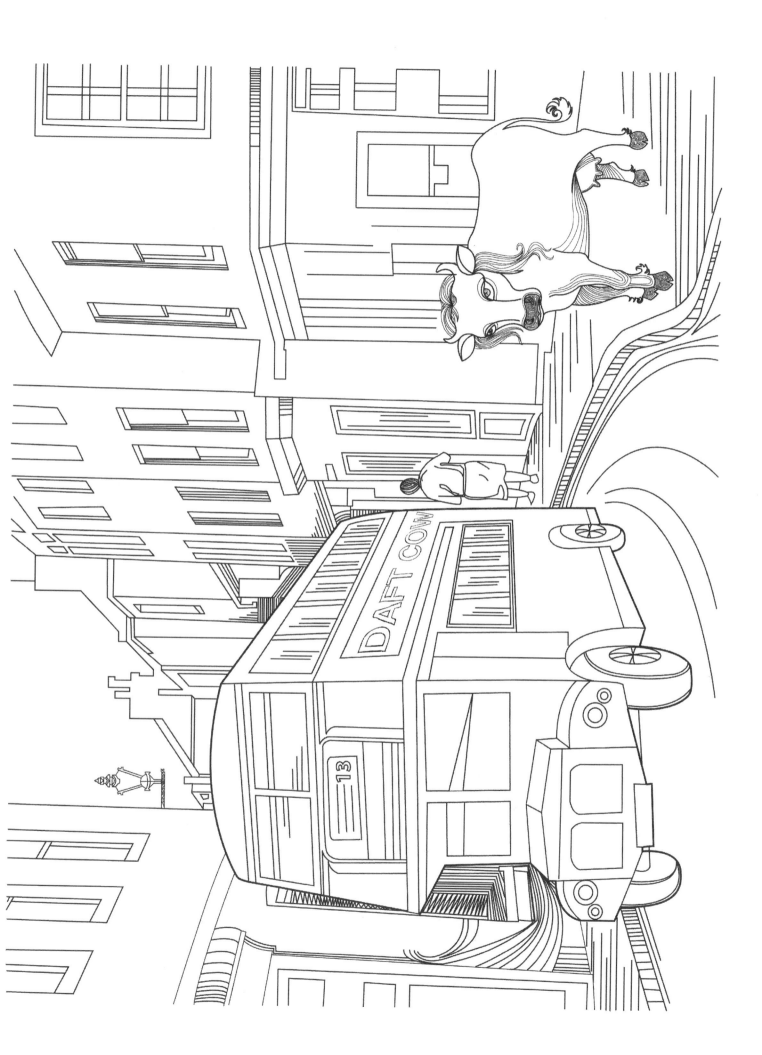

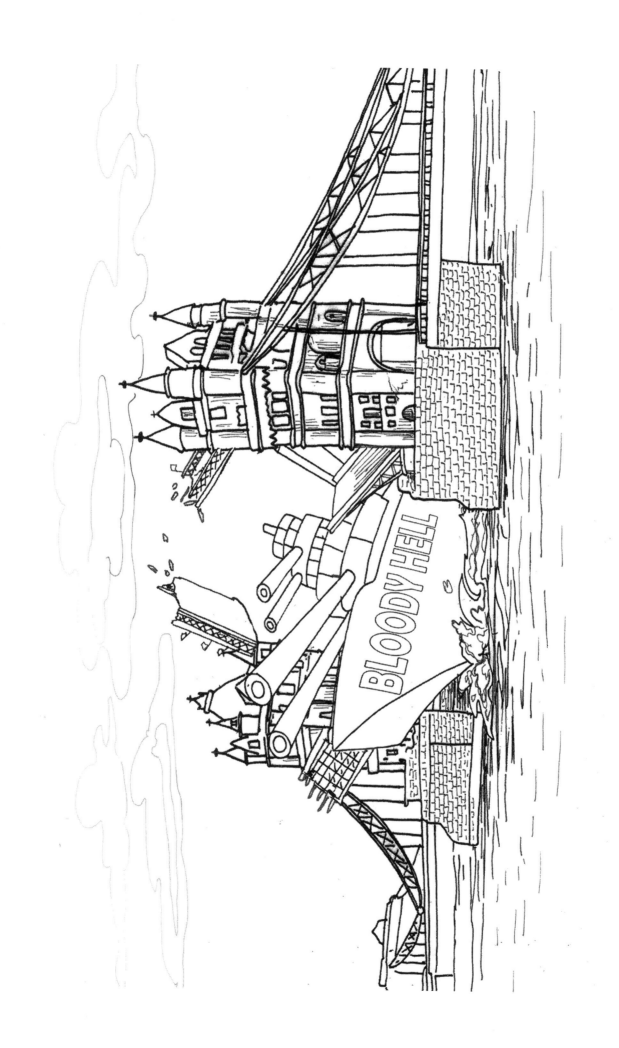

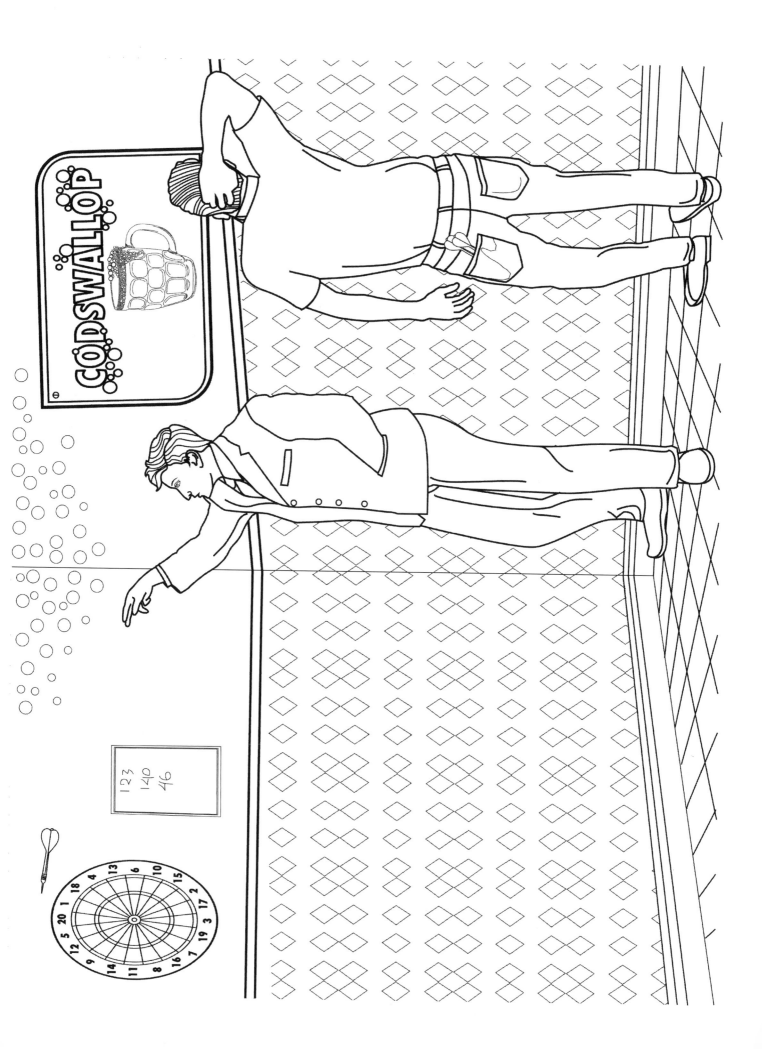

Be one of the In Crowd!

As a Mix Books Coloring Insider, you will receive FREE coloring pages to download and be among the first to know about special offers and our newest coloring books.

Sign up now, and as our thanks to you, immediately receive TEN illustrations in PDF format. Go to:

http://www.mix-booksonline.com/coloring

Join us on our facebook page:

https://www.facebook.com/coloringmix/

Other coloring books for you to enjoy:

In the Jungle: The Mighty Magical Jungle
In an Octopus's Garden: Stress Relieving Patterns
I Am Woman: A woman's coloring book to boost self-esteem and nurture self-confidence
Paisley and Patterns: Intricate Designs Coloring Book
Coloring Book for Adults: BadASS Buttocks
Coloring Book of Vintage Caricatures and Characters
Silesian Folk Tales Coloring Book: Intricate Vintage Illustrations
Coloring Book for Kids: Farm Animals
Coloring Book for Kids: Monsters
Adult Coloring Book for Relaxation: Serenity: Spirit Guides & Totems
Adult Coloring Book: Stress Relief and Relaxation: Original Hand-drawn Designs
Stress Relief Coloring Book: Patterns & Designs (Adult Coloring Books)
My Heart, My Valentine & the Color of Love: Adult Coloring Book
Adult Coloring Book: Flower Designs: Stress Relieving Patterns

Easily access all of our coloring books here:

http://www.mix-booksonline.com/category/coloring-books

74216900R00040

Made in the USA
Middletown, DE
21 May 2018